T0196440

ZARG

ZARG

COLLECTED POEMS

S A M   M U L D O O N

ZARG
COLLECTED POEMS

iUniverse books may be ordered through booksellers or by contacting:

iUniverse
1663 Liberty Drive
Bloomington, IN 47403
www.iuniverse.com
1-800-Authors (1-800-288-4677)

ISBN: 978-1-4917-9592-7 (sc)
ISBN: 978-1-4917-9593-4 (e)

Library of Congress Control Number: 2016911427

Print information available on the last page.

iUniverse rev. date: 09/16/2016

For all the cats who have owned me...

Soothsayer

Righteousness is a dud blessing
When you feel the cold, it shows
Feeding on your young is prevalent now
If the dew crystallizes the snow enfolds
The way of my life is the true spirit of love & devotion
When I see I am intuitively void
& If the expression is hampered, the soul is lost
My fear is of truth being reality
& Reality being truthful

When I'm in this body, I'm obscured
When I'm true, then I'm the angel
& When I'm open to you, I'm in blossoming quaintness
In my way, this is the first of the generation to come...

Toast

A herd of bad thoughts
Pass through my mind
Can't see my way
No more good to be seen
Is my place here at risk?
Or am I just living

An image appears to fade,
It returns, only to be false
Are you here?
Am I here?
Fortuitous place in view
Forgotten haunts seem new

At last a bright future could be at hand
Failing that, a grope in the corner is an option
A flash, then silence
A charcoal patch is all that remains...

Sam Muldoon

Day of Sadness

A lost cause to bear
A lost can of pears
A lost child on the stairs
The rest is in pairs

A lucky man on a bus
An unlucky man is one of us
He bleeds just 'cos
But unlike the lucky man, he makes no fuss

The child is found
The lucky man asks his mate round
The unlucky one loses a pound
& Revives himself with a new sound

Schtum

Smoke the plant of your garden
When does the light fade?
Inhale the essence of then
When does the dark invade?
I'm in the belly of the bear
Through the portal, I must go
Careful now, take care
Don't advise, I already know

Out to the realm of her
The height is beyond my understanding
This disorientation is only fair
Of course, the process is demanding
Without difficulty, ease wouldn't be
Oh, the fear is too much
But I go on I need to see
If only I could just touch
Milestone nirvana ahead
Wretched body gone
What I am now, need not be said

Sam Muldoon

A Request from the Owner

Do you go online?
For you I do pine
Soon you'll be mine
For all our time
We'll drink lime
I'll smoke a woodbine
& It'll be fine

The dog may whine
We'll see a sign
For somewhere selling wine
It'll be divine
WITH the divine

Combined for all time
Divine
Time
Divine
Time
No time is for me
So together, we shall see
Never will you flee
It'll be just be Me & Thee

Well that's what I see
Join me!

The Gods

Jah is my saviour
Jesus is love
Mohammed is wise
Krishna is everywhere
Buddha is almighty
Rama is eternal
Moses is king

All these are not material things
But they are what makes people sing

Generate

Generate a feeling
Feeling goes on & on
Lose out on stealing
When the night is wrong
Pacify the attack &
Chase around the back
Call for sanity is pleading
But the summer fights, then autumn cracks
So, what a night it could be
When we shall float on the feeling

Walk Away

Walk away sweet one
Come away lost one
Rest, & try not to weep
For today, is long in its pleasures
Hope is paid off by it
Rest & be glad

Going Alone

Going alone
Wanting nothing
Feeling nothing
Having friends
Having to make amends
Feeling lost
Bought at a cost
Frankly seen
Far too mean
I'm saying nothing
I'm saying something
The right road is always the hardest

Old Love's Flame

I feel her, even when she is nowhere near
To have her & beheld her beauty, so clear
Gives me wonderment of awe to look upon
A place beside me, is hers only, no other one

The days are plentiful in their beguiling rhythm
With my lady, I love to spend them
We were lovers centuries ago in simpler times
No less joyous, was our first union; it is what hath kept
our strong binds

In the passage of time, there creeps up a shadow,
where surety is doubted
Befallen become our hearts, within it's notion
That anything before today, is all that counted
Then an embrace, from skin to our very souls, rekindles
our unwavering devotion

Sam Muldoon

Flavours

I've many places to go
I've never liked Toto!
I did some Osho
I ate some Nosh(o)

I blew it with her
All to asunder
With MDF to render

Do you do all/no sports?
Do you wear red/blue shorts?
Do you drink/down shorts?
Do you attend/contempt courts

Fresh thoughts in the morning
As I said before, she'll be blinking & yawning
Do you ever find the Earth boring?
Have you heard my snoring?

I don't have all that many enemies
I don't visit many cemeteries
I believe in meant-to-be's
I have to pay rent for keys

Blind to our followers
Don't watch the borrowers
Listen to all foreigners
We all meet coroners

Jest about the big master plan
Make jelly lemon flan
Catch me if you can
Take 'em out with a pan

Reasonable testing behaviour
Are you meant to be my saviour?
I'm not much braver
I'm not going to shave her

To the top of that big hill
Take another triangular pill
Seasoning done, with some dill
Grow them on your windowsill
Tell me now; have you had your fill?
Or are you just gunning for that Phil
I'm always one to kill time
I'm just a worker at the mill
Dress in shabby clothes all the time
Don't force me to drink cheap wine
I'll smoke any kind of woodbine
I know it's not quite my time

It's just the way we have to be
We have many many sights to see
Call me for some tea
Do you really want rid of me?
I've got a hell of a lot to do
I like to hear birds going "coo"
Do you sing on the loo?
Did you hear that pig go "moo"?
Singular in the trend of things
I've not had that many flings
I know it's awful, when he sings
We could be better at these things

I've got a lot of useless possessions
I never go to any confessions
I always apply my concessions
We all have multi-faceted connections
I have too many of these things
She makes my hair stand on end, when she sings
Santa is the one who does that he brings things
In this world, where there aren't enough kings

Causeways are for cars
Drinks are for bars
Kingdoms are for Czars
Kids are for Ma's

Keys are for doors
Spots are messed up pores
I kiss your open sores
I turn the radio off, when I hear the bores

Have you had lessons learnt?
Have you worked for what you've earned?
Look at the toast you've burnt
Back I've come, returned

Pick up all those pieces
Give me & me for all my theses
You'll always be a good sis'&
It'll be being with you, that I'll miss

Divine in the Time of Blasphemy

The colour is lost from the view
Then a hand taps the screen
These things are not new
To be awake, is not to be mean
This city is on the verge
We're not sure of what
The band blasts out a heavy dirge
& In their song they claim to be on top

If you were to be in the same place
Then maybe it would be this
The man is at the top & he's aced
The way there, is a swizz
But he earned it, with his own talent
The press have their way
& The bird nearby the screen, sings its lament
The reporters are on their way

The screen is blank & he sees the image of himself.
Burned in his mind
The memory is so disgusting; he feels the urge to do
the pluck
The way of his heart is drenched, with the guilt of the
time of kind
It's what started this, when he really didn't give a f**k

The door slows down in the opening, for a quick glance
from the outside
The room is now dark
Then, a blast of light, as the door is opened from the
left side
The view is now stark
He sees this playing in his mind, as he recalls...

The light is to the right he flicks the switch
The door ahead is blue & shiny
The way forward is clear
The present is beside the bed
& He retreats to the study
The laptop is on & connected
He begins to write...

"...Tonight we sing for the old
The day is gone & it's time to relax
We should like to think this way & be bold
The rhyme will tell you the facts

I be tha man, ov da big style
I'm a lyrical murderer, of the highest degree
If you be checkin' dis, add the CD to your pile
When you hear tha beat I've made,
You'll wanna feel free, If you be in da place
Yaw ass is getting' torn apart, with a Mutha F'in
briefcase attack..."

End of Loves Embrace

I'm here again
The place of no speed, or direction
I'm lost in the sadness &
I'm feeling ALL pain
Together we may be better
But on our own, we could be much weaker
I feel that you're here with me
In that same state

Today I felt like I was in a rut
I was in turmoil
Hardly noticing the weather
Or the people
Now I feel you near
Even though, you're not

Soon, I say soon
We shall be in sweet union
Until then
Sleep tight my love

Beyond It

Trap to be mixed up in
Throw your tabs in the bin
Fill yourself with sin
Tell everyone about your kin

Buy a good ring
Listen to the machine go: ding!
Then it goes: ping!
Have a little wingding

Dress for the date
Look at what I ate
Make them your mate
Go out with Kate

Slap on the cream
Look at your wooden beam
Tear & cut the seams
Go beyond your means

Toddler

Nobody around
Nobody here
Nobody wants
To hear the tears

Flesh of a clown's
I'm feeling down
In my nightgown
I'm turning brown

Do you make a key?
I need a pee
Does it free me?
I'm only three

Sam Muldoon

Sight

Do you know me?
I'm good to thee
I do it for free
I wish I was still three
It's the way to be

Do you know Ste?
Are you afraid of a bee?
Are you going to go to zee?
Do you, like me, hate the fee?
I've got a big key
& it's all in your wee
Don't you ever see?

Sleepynessness

Oh to sleep, oh to dream
'Tis but cupid calling
On this night, we shall conquer
For all these days, are blissful
Today is always the right time
Together we are magic
But loneliness awaits me
But apart, in limbo, we doth stay
Nectarine drinks, can appease us
& Make us want a new Jesus
But again, I sigh & say goodbye
For a messiah
Is all too meaningless

Progression is a Must

Walk by my side
Not on tow
Pass a truck that's wide
Fake having a blow

Joke about it all
Jest & twirl
Come prancing, with a ball
Blow chunks & hurl

Fly away in your mind
Dream, love, die & return
Don't be with just your kind
Come back around & you'll have money to burn
Laugh at misfortune
Cry at good times
Snigger at loss of fortune
Collapse in good lyrical rhymes

Sam Muldoon

Outward 2 U

Feel the joy of peace
Look not on the pedestal, but underneath
My interest will never cease
Watch out, as the wickedness is increased
When the moment is gone
Revisit the future, for the plan
Don't find out where you're from
True beauty, is within a person
If I'm around, notice me there
Look to my thoughts
& Not, my underwear
Compassion, not lust, is what I've brought

Coverdale in the press
The need, is in my seed
I cannot say, what I want to express
Maybe it's between the lines, U need 2 read
Stop your sorrow
It's time to feed

Down Further

Sorrow passes by slow
It's just something I know
I wish they wouldn't go
But they do, & I flow

Losses increasing
Wardens policing
No wars ceasing
Hope decreasing

New flesh for old
Chin up, be bold
The whole world sold
My hand is crap, so I fold

Life is always there
They always end up bare
They just don't have a care
This just isn't fair

Sam Muldoon

Ho-Hum

I fear nothing
But I am frightened by nothing
Is this possible?
Me thinks so...
I am not afraid
But I am - of nothing
So I know, that *something*
Is not to be wary of
But NOTHING
Is the worst possible thing
In my senses

If everyone was like this
We would be too boring
& Laugh at a moment
With death at hand
Now, I know, this wouldn't do

Forget the pain &
Kiss the rain

Hinder Me Not

A call is made to the tribe
A warning is hindered, is a warning needed
For I can still see, & this, is myself in ruins
No loss is greater than mine
In this, I do wallow
My face is falling slowly down
Soon I shall expire
& Cease to be a part of it
If I stay with it
I shall be drained
Then forever be, a useless oddity

This is my scenario, & I believe, in my way
Because without my own way
I'd be nobody
I know, I am somebody
So forget the tribe
I'll stick to mine own, & then
I shall be me!

Sam Muldoon

Do We?

Do we know her?
Do we show her?
Do we blow him?
Do we bring it?
Do we go in?
Do we throw it in the bin?
Do we recognise the sin?
Do we fulfil it?
Do we have to sit?
Do we have to knit?
Do we have to sh*t?
Do we have to watch?
Do we have any scotch?
Do we mean what we say?
Do we keep it at bay?
Do we all turn gay?
Do we all talk to K?
Do we work with J?
Do we have to pay!
Do we all know?
Do we all go?
Do we all throw?
Do we all glow?
Do we all sew?
Do we all show?

Define It

A breath, is fulfilling for all
A blink, is all the sleep I need
A sigh, slows my feeling
A cough, is liberating
A sneeze, is an orgasm
A fall, is mesmerising
A belch, is my toxic waste
A chew, is my occupation
A knife, is my salvation

&...

A kiss, is my gift
Please accept

Sam Muldoon

Duct Flow

A dribble down the cheek
It flows so easily
The beads increase
They fall faster & faster
Soon there will be a puddle
But such things, don't hinder
All the liquid comes from the windows
& a torrent of sniffles aid it
So it seems, to be this sad
The gist is understood
& The pearls fall from the wood
Soon, I'll be calling it a flood

A light beckons to be seen
But the mood is too mean
If I were a duck
With them I would preen

Please be more than this...

Sequential

I see your waist
& I see your lashes
Real evolution in haste
I see you at social bashes
The way for us, is unclear
I wish I had you, in my presence
I hope, to feel you near
& Shower you with presents
If you take up my offer
Will there be a touch on the skin?
I see the voice you have, is softer
Than most, of whom I'm akin to
Will you see me in the sky, waving to greet you?
& Will my name be on your lips frequent?
I'm all good & ready to meet you
& With my spirit, I will thus sequence

A flow of the arm
To help us disarm
From the needs of the now
& The stinging sweat of the brow
Can only remind of harm
But will not cause alarm
In this respect, we do bow
It's up to you now

Sam Muldoon

All We Do, All We Achieve

Call up one of the spirits
Go along & do it
You'll get through it
& You'll have time to sit
Wait!
Hold that!
I didn't mean it!

Let's start again & brew it
& We'll both get through it
Jump around & move it
Have a rest & another sit
I don't like this, one little bit

Maybe soon, I'll have a fit
& I'll be wearing all of my kit
All together, we'll finish it
We won't be having a fit
We could write a little ditty about it
Anyway, we do it we'll renew it
& They won't say we blew it
They'll say, we got through it
& I'll be proud of it
It'll be a big achievement, won't it?

They'll stand back & appreciate it
They'll like it, more than a little bit
They'll hopefully love it
& Then we'll be above it
& We'll have to cover it
Then present it
Then clean it
&
WE MEAN IT

Imperfect Greenhouse

Feel it coming
It can be numbing
Live in a pot
Could be something that it's not
Turning towards the sun
Continue wishing for fun
Try to scream out
It's impossible, without a doubt
You're just a plant!
& Your tub is on a slant

Friday Night In

Have a cake here
Stay awake there
Lost in the passion
Dress just for fashion

Praise the night time
Haze on the skyline
Nothing is lost
Love has no cost

Homeless Pauper

Numb & old
Out in the cold
Never acting bold
Your life's sold
You broke the mould
You're in a hold
So you'll have to fold

Through Snow

Feeling all gone over, the white cliffs of Dover
I'm not in a mower; I'm a slow grower
A stitch & sew-er, I'm not going to blow her
But I'll definitely know her

Let's ride with the flow
Go on, have a go
Do a long throw

Then...

You'll soon know
Which way to go
Through...

All
This
Snow

Contemplate

For the day, I see light
For the night, I see lament
In the wake, for you, I'll fight
Not one, who just came & went
In the tide, many things float
In our mind, this does wonder
If you were near, around us, I'd build a moat
To make us grow fonder
If you'd see, I'll be me
If you'd smell, I'll be stronger
If you'd look, you'll surely see
If you'd sniff, it'll be a good pong
When I'm near, YOUR heart does bounce
When I'm far, I'm close to YOUR side
If you're near, MY heart does bounce
When you're far, you're close to MY side
So if it's right, then let's join forces & see
That's if you'd feel right tonight
Or soon, we shall see...

Sam Muldoon

Generate Regeneration

Now to sleep
Be kind, & try not weep

Jest & play in time
Listen to that phat rhyme

Don't stop to avoid
I'm not F'in paranoid!

Clean in my head
"POO" - Drop Dead Fred!

I'm in sync with my psyche
Give me a race on a bikey

Flash my parts to her
Une Oui, Une Fleur

One Yes, One Flower
Now, I'll recharge my power

Interpretation Xenon

Fate has no deviation
I won't try to save this nation
What's the plan for salvation?
The end of creation?

If the pests were clean
I could be mean
Chaos likes his beer &
I am here

When does my clock stop?
Does time have a map?
Okay, do I run till I drop?
Clean up the mess with a mop

The way to me, is hard
But the process is natural
There is no façade
Listen to the caterwaul

When you reach me, you'll see
Then you don't be
What is it in me?
Why 'tis thee!

When you live, you learn
When you love, you adorn
The crown of the stubborn
Just push the little button
When is it time, for now?
Now, then again, now
No "Wow!" for that go

Sam Muldoon

I'm in the mood of Kudrow
I'm feeling true colours
I'm looking for those above us
Come dear, under the covers
It's just wives & lovers

I feel in no rush
To touch the bush
Or eat the mush
No, not on the bus!
When I see her in my mind
All my thoughts are kind
If I could ever find her
I'll hopefully bind
Flies around the place
But my part is over
On to the next lover
&
No

It's not over...

Intent in Love

I can see all that is beauty
I feel everything that is there
I know all that could be
I taste a whim within

For them, mine is open
Between night & day
I crawl into slumber
A peace is all around, & within me

A zest for the feeling
An urge to caress
My search for a meaning
I find, is too much at best

So, I soon do dwell at your gate
No contract of intent is made
We relax and enslave ourselves, in fate
I'm sure this won't be a memory that fades

Jet-Set, Jed-Met

For us it is set
No more ways to go
Forward, but never out
Doubt is in my nature
To us, it is our saviour
To feel is to live
To live, is to feel &
To know is to die
For death, is the only way through
Another way to play
Is soon forgotten
Lost in the hustle
& Remembered in the day
If we're really alive
Then we must be all
Because, now, to live
It is to BE, & when you BE, you are ALL
Nothing is lost in the passing
Only the memory

Midweek

Wednesday is gone
What did go on, upon?
Who's the don?
He must be a one

Fred was told
He acted bold
Poker player folds
Hot water scolds

Manifold of stars
Papas & Mamas
Drive their kids in cars

Don't cha know dat?
I wear a hat
I won't ever be phat
Cos there ain't a dip...
Where I just sat

Apprehension

I'm not content with you
You sometimes call me a fool
What did you think?
That I'd got the wrong tool?
Why aren't you here with me, winding the spool?
What happens to all the people in number two?
Are they gonna speak down to you?

Sam Muldoon

Fortunately

Dis all those people
Climb up the steeple
Meet & have a tipple
Cut off your nipple
Talk with Robert Fripp
Give him some jip
Break into her hip
Quick to sip
Don't call me again!
Build a solid den
Watch a wren
Learn about Zen
Link is the place
Something is ace
I walk at a fast pace
I'm back on the case
Call me now
Meet & bond
Dress as a con
Middle of my brow
Is where you'll find me
It's the only way to be
All out, & free

Give ME the key

Demanding

If we seem too nice
We get the opposing treatment
Rough justice prevails
And abandonment is forthcoming

A loss of hope turns
To agonising chirpiness &
All my bad is cleaned

Together we're in the union of spirit
I may become addicted to your power
But soon I shall be whole again
Without you

Loneliness is apparent &
Fear is all there is to think
Could we be?
Or, will we be?

Your choice

Falling Over the Street

False joy inside
True boy outside
Babyish talk
Slapdash walk

Funny quip
About a lemon dip
Nasty taste of malt
Big door to bolt
The rhythm is gone
Remedy: eat a scone

Fool the Few

Beat is good enough
Rest is for the best
Nest is for the birds
Time for the words
Tables for the nerds
Grass for the herds
Seconds for the thirds
Recuperate & renew
Could be for the few
I feel brand new
Quick, pull up a pew
Stand in the queue
Take in the view
Cows go "moo"
I go "coo"
Oh phew!

Sam Muldoon

We Must Know

Forced out in the end
I've got something to bend
Are you going to the old bar?
Are you falling into an old bra?
Do you think he still can?
What's the problem?
Aren't you alone?
Can you stop them?
Aren't you whole?
When are you vain?
Where are you in pain?
Do you see that frame?
It's broken, & you're the one to blame
Do you have any shame?
Look, you must die out the flame!
& Chuck it down the drain

Together

We stand together
What's in the weather?
I'm at the end of my tether
I'm as light as a feather
Are we together?
Are we together?
We are now here...
We are now HERE
Where are we now?
Well, WE ARE HERE...
Together or not?
Together to rot
As close as what?
Forget thee not
We were together...
Now, we are lost in the nether
Tortoise

Monday's fresh start
Tuesday we'll never part
Wednesdays for a dare-e
Thursday is for art
Friday always fart
Saturday for Bart
Sunday is a tart

Sam Muldoon

Future Quotes

Together we will conquer
The ties of the law led society
But the fundamental things are like:

Don't mess with my tea &
Don't force them to be

Eternality

To do is retarded fear
To see is skilful journeying
To know, is peril &
To be is unworthiness

If I doubt, I'm sane
If I find, I grunt, I grin & smile
When I bleed, I settle
When I touch, I reveal my sense

The sound is my partner &
The fresh, is my nature
Divide the experience &
Flow to the room, of your eternality

Serenity

Cluster in an apple tree
Bunch of useless keys
Fresh & as quick as them Bumble Bees
I'll bring them to their knees
They might be quick to appease
But I'll blast them, with a sneeze

Go around town listening to snooze
Giving up & going on to have some booze
Coming back & hearing the news
I don't know anyone that lives in The Mews
But don't do it, when standing in queues
I'm not one to blow a fuse

Sam Muldoon

Solution

Feast on the vibration
The nodes of inner contemplation
Forever in the realm of spirit
Never a need to fear it
Hasten not, for it shall come
Take it as a rule of thumb
Vestibule of a notion
Joy unbound, like an ocean
Be together & within it
Load up your wares - your kit
Ride with us, for ill will be undone
I'm sure it'll be fun
Drink a psychoactive potion
Become fluid in your motion

Run, Jump, Fly & Be Fit!

Celebrate, to get through it
Soon, I'm sure, you'll see them
You don't know exactly when
It's the natural evolution
With a positive, full fruition...
No Ego, No Fear, IS The Solution!

Back In a Mo

Back in a Mo...
Talk to Moe
Av a go
Say "So!"
Salsa
Rasa
Bassa
Massa
Mi Casa
Su Casa
Mondo Bassa
A Good Lass
Drink Bass
See Cas
Sassafras
Lasses
Molasses
Honey
Cane
Demerara
Brown
Golden Syrup
Dextrose
Sucrose
Glucose

Splutter

I'm here for a long time
If I lose, I will be fine

A forest of dreams
Will soon collide with an action
For now, is all there is
& Then, will always be then

Tomorrow can never be reached
So don't look there for your answers
Look to the moment & be there
For whatever you do, you will be guided
& Truly we do follow this

For NOW is the time
Live it

Love it

& BE!

Inauguration

Destiny awaits me
I'll have to wait & see
Is it you?
Or is it me?
I've got the key &
So's haves thee
Match, it's gonna be
I'll make you see
I'll drink my tea
Then I'll do over a pea
Kill it with my teeth
Then bury it, underneath
Do I have to breathe?
It makes my mood seethe
It's all in the weed
It's all I need
I won't bleed
I'll put in the seed &
Make some mead
I'm all clued up
I'm gonna sup, sup, sup
Live it up
Start again
Without pain
I'll tame &
It'll be me to blame
What a shame, so inane
Wash his mane
Lay down claim
Don't be to blame
Just cane
Fly Jane, Fly...

One for the Diary

Glory time is giggly years
I'm sure she has the greatest thighs
I'm sure she's not eating pies
Or killing any flies

She looks to the sky, for her beloved
But she's now, as old as Old Mother Hubbard
I know she's locked in a cupboard
Old Mother Hubbard, not my beloved

Chaos

Song-lines & treacherous actions
The island over there, has many factions
Do you know she couldn't understand fractions?
But was highly impressed with fractals

Reaction Oeuvre

I feel no more love
I feel less than zero
I am not allowed
For this is yesterday &
Tomorrow is not now
We all wish
That this, was not true
But I AM here
Is this a point to note
Or is it pointless
I Am All
I Am One
We Are All
We Are One
Did you know these things?
Did I know?
Too soon to dwell on
Too loud to hear
All is real to all
A fall is followed by
A trip into... Minds eye
From which we learn
From which we see
I'm in this now
I'm feeling the real thing
It's not good for me
It's no good for anyone
It's all &...
It's FATE
So you should see
It's just how it is, no more, no less
Keep me here keep me here
I'm not well enough for love
Given OR received, Lost OR gained
Today is only going to be yesterday soon
So do your worst...
Mutha F'in' Daddy!

Sam Muldoon

Quirky

Peace be with you
Peace be with you
Arrest them all
Put 'em against the wall
Then have a ball
Do you know my call?
In the American fall
America will fall &
We'll have it all &
A brand new ball gown
I'll be getting down & dirty
At thirty, go Berty! Be Nerty (Nerty?)
Be flirty, Murk, Burk, Quirk, Shirk?
Tallness

Fear, queer, near, oh dear, oh my, a pie…
In the sky
Remember that
What a twat
I'm in a hat &
I'm a cat, with a bat
End is a rat
I'll eat you, Mr. Ball
Against the wall, I'm not tall…
…At all

Upper Classes

Insider dealings
Strange feelings
Potty people
No steeple

Driver's wage
Butler's age
Growing plants
Killing ants

All these & more
Are millionaires' chores

The View

The night sings, to your voice pattern
You feel the way, to know it
If I'm here, I'm not there
When there's love, there's also hate
If you breed, you have a purpose &
If you blink, you will dream

The way is up &
The view is splendid

Sam Muldoon

Ditty for a Loony

I'll have to leave it at that
You'll soon be having a tattoo of a bat
You might get a chance to see the cat
I will, of course, never be fat
You know, I'm gonna beat you with my hat
I've just wasted my time, as if I've just sat

Just More

What's on your mind?
Are you very kind?
Do you like to unwind?
What did you find?

Are you in pain?
Do you act vain?
Do you go & blame?
Do you feel shame?

Bliss Inside

Come away from the heat
Try to be a bit more neat &
I'll give you a treat
Not consisting of meat
Do you live in this street?
Do you know where, he'd said we'd meet?
Does your baby suck a teat?
Or does he use a seat?
I'd like to come to your place
Then I'd really get on the case
It'd be so ACE
We'd go at it, at a fast pace
Dress up in each others clothes &
Hope it soon snows
They'll say: "That's the way love goes"
I'll rub & massage your toes
Do you have green eyes?
Do you travel the skies?
Do you eat many pies?
Do you know when it dies?
If you hadn't thought of this
It'd be them you'd miss
I'll leave you now
With a metaphorical kiss
& A momentary hiss...

Sam Muldoon

Changing Room Drama

You danced till you fell over
You were seen at Hark to Rover
You left over your leftover
You blessed a field of clover
I went out to the shed
I knew it was dead
It wasn't red
"Beep-Beep", is all it said

She went over the sky
She could fly
She made 'em all wonder why
She killed him with a pie
He thought he was IT
He wasn't a complete shit
He knew it would fit
He would sew & knit
Now, does it fit?
Go on, &...?
Fall on a wall, fly on a pie
Quickly do you die
Slow do you go
Nicely do you flow
Rushing in the snow

First Request

Treat me with kind &
You'll feel me right
Taste the morning in mind &
It'll help you through the night

Bless the moment of joy
Stand near & feel the warmth
Shape of land ahoy
An island of delights, to raunch

A time of conversing
A place to be
Galaxies of emotions traversing
A way to see
If you listen to the silence
They're is no need for vigilance
We live by crosses & noughts
Along the avenue of fantasy, we do stroll
Into depths of a shared experience
A taste of each other's soul
It's not something I've felt since...
...Last season, it was another
But now, we're in that zone
Will you be my lover?
Or do you want to be alone?

Sam Muldoon

Question

Too much of the sweetest
In a way that's just the most
Beauty is simply the cut above the rest
The one whom should butter my toast
Resting in the wake for a time
Arise again & I'm doing fine
Lest nor we do shine
Woulds't thou be mine?

Process of Evolution

Heal your spirit & combine your life
Be the most-est, feel the toasties
Crush the fear, swell the breath &
Feel the life think the difference
Sink to the self & dwell there with me
Find the gratitude, feel the touch of love
Grab the time & savour with joy
Feel the insides grow, taste the rhythm &
Steal the instance forever
If you do, then you are in my zone
Of blissful juxtaposition
When you're there, be with me
Then together we'll consider & resign, to self
Then the feeling will be all ours
For evermore

Thursdays

Having a meal, having to keel over
Knowing the road, knowing the code over
Wanting to know, having the way home
Wanting to see, never to play away

Death in the clan
Nothing, but a flash in the pan
Relax & unwind
We are far too kind

Mayfly

Skin on hands, sweat on palms
For the ultimate charms, go for the demands
Little do we know, much we do say
It is now the month of May

Sam Muldoon

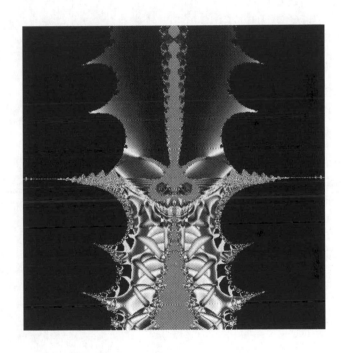

Garden of Eden

Fresh thoughts of you
The memories are unclear
But the sentiment is strong
I see you in lilac
I feel you close
When you do come
In the centre of my mind
Is the union of us
For, it is to be true
I'm sure
But all is time to wait, time to relax &...
Let it happen, if I'm wrong, then I'm...
Dreaming, dreaming of what should be
Dreaming of our love, forever love
Pure love
Iridescence around you
Pure, shining, white fire
Which nothing can dampen
I don't fear anything
Not even the inevitable
For
It
Shall
Be

Flowers of purity & divinity
Within us both
Surrounding & enveloping
Petals of empathy & compassion
Seeds of new life, at the centre
Stem of natural resonance
Leaves of protection
Roots of knowledge
Sap of soul nutrition &
The colour of serenity
In common, these, have we
For together, we make up
The companion
To the tree

Street Scene

Hypnotise the wretch, a set of orders to go
Tragedy awaits the unsuspecting &
A fully done task, is hindered in that wake

Now we're close, too many clichés
Too many lost children &
All around there is nothing
A cane is not accepted & she fell over
In a bigger way, for this, we now do heed this
"'Tis but a folly my dear"
He sneers & turns away
The last is over &
The old day begins

Sam Muldoon

Oceania

The fame of beauty is odd
But when it catches you, then revel
If the within is your God
Then you could be on the right level

I'm in this world of time
The love I feel, is all messed up
There is no need to give a sign
Because the truth isn't dressed up

A map of love, is what I desire &
The instigator was very near
Don't be afraid of hatreds fire
The map & the fire are holding the rear

I want the touch of human affection
For the need, overrides the notion
Please don't make me lose my direction
Because sorrow, can be an ocean

When I find my way to exaltation
I'll be in the hearts of the whole nation

Lend me your force
For the reason of euphoria
In my actions I have no remorse
Listen to the sweet boy sing "Gloria"
A faint smile curls my lips &
A light flickers in my eyes

When the final contact clicks &
The last horseman rides

Occurrences

In the days of our union
It will be the greatest feeling
The walls will be hot &
The floor will be our hay

When the birds sing, we'll hear the music
If the clouds pass over, we'll feel the chill &
Move closer for our warmth
When the night comes
We'll shine &
When you come to me
Time will stand still &
We will sigh

Sam Muldoon

Yours

Today is upon me
I feel the morning creeping in
The night has now ended
If you live for the dawn
You have good love
When the shadows appear
The sun is prevalent
The day is all yours
Useless conclusion

Not to be is too much
So we be
Not to say is okay
So we stay schtum

Not to see is my way
So we blink
Not to feel is right on
So we show our fingers
Not to know is their ignorance
So we think
Not to walk is a poor way
So we stagger
Not to eat is stupid
So we gorge
Not to drink is more stupid
So we gulp
Not to write is fine
So we stop

Unnamed

Warm my head
For it's gone now
We feel all
We fail to scale the wall

I'm in deaths embrace
You're in my special place
Soon to fade
Too much room to be afraid
Now is your chance
This ain't no circumstance

Feel the blue
Get your due
Forget sanity
Plead for vanity

We're lost in a limbo
I've killed the window

Sam Muldoon

Butterfly's Fate

Falling down my way
No? Well, whatever
What did you say?
Are you ready to stay?
Always, come what may

Be brave in your word
Can't be what I'd heard
Just me, when I erred
Are you outside, little bird?

Fern in the wind
All the new ideas binned
Not all were killed & pinned
Just the millions who'd sinned

The Best Yet

Wear some blue feathers
Fiddle with the weathers
Let's have a get-together
Go along with Heather

Call on your on your old man
He'll tell you, "You Can"
He'll not put on a ban
We'll open a can

Don't let the wax wane
Or you'll go insane &
With that, there's a lot of pain
All of your energy will drain

Go out with your woman
Tell her, "I'm just comin'"
Later you might be humming
But make sure,
You don't leave the water running
Have a good time, while you're out
Have your girlfriend do her famous pout
Drink up all the glorious stout
Wobble down the street
With a twist & a shout
Fall in love with your best friend
It'll turn sour in the end &
They'll drive you round the bend
The could force you
To have extra bills to send

Sam Muldoon

Give up on a holiday
Forget about a holy day
Just collect your hard earned pay &
Announce to the room, that you're not gay

Finally in this poem
You'll learn about doing &
Your knowledge will be growing
Many good things are coming

No Answer

My happiness dwindles
My spirit is drained
All my thoughts are thick with hatred
Why is this so?
Why are we suffering?
When I speak, do I lie?
When I hear, am I deaf?

Soon all these will be forgotten
& We'd shrug & carry on with this grind
Not just a daily task
Not to use the oxygen mask
Severance is needed
& The bind will be broken
As we drift into sleep
The demon comes alive
& The fantasy begins
Soon enough, is not acceptable here
We need more that this
& I'll wait for your waking greeting
'Cos we're in the same state
Both in word, manifestation & sorrow...

No more do we smile
No more do we laugh
This is REAL!
& This has no way to leave us
Tomorrow is not where we should be
But, however we battle it
This is where we end up
So NOW
Is irrelevant
& Then, is IT!

My sarcophagus is full
& I am empty

Sam Muldoon

Old Man of the Hill

Follow him along by the watchtower. Forgive him, for he doesn't know the strength of his power. All the time he walks along the animals around him cower & the village people have all (but one) turned sour. His quest is for a peaceful life. Sitting at home with his beloved wife, they always get on there is no strife. She cuts up his steak with her knife. Yesterday he came across a dead rabbit, & for it's sake, he buried it, that was one of his habits. He ponders over his humble funds, & has to add to it, 'twas a strange day, & just by coincidence his name is Babbitt. For a long while now, he would walk around the cliffs & for the sake of it; he would shower his local pub landlord with many gifts. A long while ago there was a gold rush, & many of them sifted, no one got rich from it, & many off them were left miffed. His old dog was long gone now & has a monument of a cross. He realised early on in his relationship with it, that it was the boss & his wife really DID give a toss, not like most people, they worshipped people like the long gone pop star dross, If you watched him long enough you would see that he seldom blinked & when corresponding to his family, he used a nib that was inked. On thing that he despised were those whom wore coats that were mink. He journeyed on a liner one summer & it did, just sink. I found out about this man through a website, for some strange reason I searched for a kite, I emailed many companies & only got one bite, which was from him, & found him to be quite bright. On a Wednesday he collects his mail & takes up a very large pail to fill with dew water, for his...Whale, which is only a baby & is not for sale. Some day he'll get a bite whilst fishing & just for now, he'll just have to keep on wishing. It's too important, the things he's missing, but all the rest of the village keep on dismissing him. His new dog isn't called Shep or Sam, it's called Jeff & just like all other dogs he's got smelly breath. His age is a large number, & he's profoundly deaf, & was a friend to a cat called Seth. On a Monday he walks two miles to the post office to get his & his wife's pension, & their weekly edifice, & then he goes to the mini-market & insists that they help him control Jeff's fits with a tonic. He enjoys his daily walks & is quite fit. Afterwards he has tea & a long sit, & if Jeff is lucky he gets a juicy titbit. He opens emails & afterwards, he has to "Quit".

Hope Turning to Despondency

Come dance
Come prance
Take the same stance
Let's go to France

Sun is evil
Like a tiny weevil

Moon is calm
Apply more balm

Distant Whispers
Close sisters
Many misters
I've kissed hers
I've got blisters
Too many "Aster La Vistas"
Left for dead
No one heard what I said

Lean Over

Squelch in effect
Talk of the peach
Rest & be content
This is all well & done
No fun, just gloominess
& I need it soon

What?
You may ask
But why?
I may say
This, my concubine
Forever isn't too long
For now it's not bad
Tomorrow is here
Beer & more beer
So unloved
In confined now
Indecisive then
Feel my heat
Dress in peach &
Test the meal
How is it that we feel?
My spirit is now out of reach

Sam Muldoon

Not Sooooo Clear

My conscientiousness is now open
The doors of perception are alive
Catch the Flibs, and rope them
My hope is that they survive

To me all I know is known
A frozen quote
Doth I speak...
My world is where I roam
This like makes me meek
If the window was open
Then I'd see the light
When a thought is frozen
It's vulnerable to a knife
Then I twist and fall
If you're around here
My glass could be tall
& My state would be fear

Paranoid Owner

Walk through a wood
He says, "I only wish I could"
Cat called Buddy
Top with a hood
Demon with blue blood
Doesn't act like he
Should back inside the wood
There's a lot of mud
This phone is a dud
Oh, I wish you would
Call me soon
I'm no longer a loon
You came too soon
I only want the moon to go with it...
What's it? Says it
Where I sit
What's it? Says it
Where I fit

What's it?

Sam Muldoon

Q &...

When does the soul think?

How does the clock know?

Who does the ground belong to?

What does the sea say?

Why does the bird sing?

When can the moon sleep?

How can the curtain draw?

Who do the blind see?

What can the phone hear?

When can the line end?

Soon Love

Society is all so contrived
I don't know how I've survived
I could have just cried
But I know you're on my side
Ignorance is what I can't abide
They all have time to bide
It's not all in my mind
It's not at all kind
What is it, I'll find...
In the depths of your mind?

Fabio

Fallen angels of hope
Travelling along a rope
Going out with time
Drunk too much wine
Fascinate a crowd

This is the answer
I'm still a dancer

High Blues Hue

Bad things are due
Things are in a shade of blue
Is this the right hue?
Does she still have the flu?
Cool! I'm in
With my cheeky grin
I like to win
Sometimes with sin
Blessed with a gift
Causes no rift
Flour ready sieved
She's left miffed

So am I...

When we see, we touch
If we breathe, we get soul
When we bleed, we flow
If we jump, we fly
When we eat, we take it in
If we smile, we know
Feathers are of lizards &
Scales are our skin
A fish sees us in our essence &
A bird sees us in our clumsiness

I see to touch
I bleed to flow
I eat to take it in
And I know, when I smile

Afternoon

We are best within it
I certainly don't fit
I'm not one to just sit
But I've got all the kit
Less is better
More is wetter
Read my Letter
1st prize Red Setter

Pages of my book
Some that they took
Lollipop to suck
Talking to a crook

Did it end?
Did they defend?
But, I did send
Oh right...

...The End.

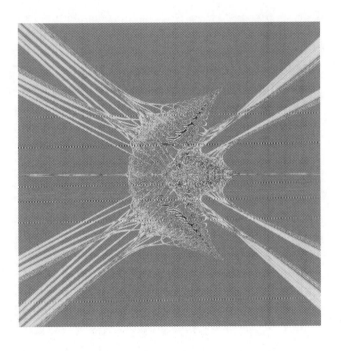

Printed in the United States
By Bookmasters